Soul Notes

By Jarrin Wooten

Copyright © 2012 Author Name

All rights reserved.

ISBN:

DEDICATION

To every creator whose story is yet to be told, create anyway

Contents

Note To Self 1
Creator 2
Excuses 3
Torn 4
Self Love 5
Learning Curve pt. 2 6
Obligated 7
Law of Averages 8
Self Care 9
Listen 11
Guilt Trip 12
Less Is More 14
Betrayal's Interlude 15
The Key 17
Innergy 18
This Is Americkkka 19
Footage of A Fallen People 20
Love Drunk 22
Grammar 101 23
Manifest 24
All In 25
Inaudible 26
The Great Compromise 27
Make Change 29
War Stories 30
9:40 PM 31
Call Casting 32
9:21 AM 33
Grammar 101 pt. 2 34
Disconnect 35
Insomniac 36
Picture Perfect 37
Sensitive 38
#2 39
Genesis 1:29 40
Needs 41
OCD 42
Comfort 43
'16 Pessimist 44
Weight 46
Reassure 47
Baggage Claim 48

Integration 49
Understanding 50
Redemption 51
Still 53
Ironic 54
11:49 PM 55
Need Me 56
Unattainable 57
Up 58
Red Pill 59
Friend Zone 60
A Virtue 62
Twisted 63
Domestic Terrorists 64
Balance 65
Bad Day 66
50/50 67
Take Time 68
Love Too Fast 69
Stay Woke 70
IDK 72
Let's Get Married 73
Forgiveness 74
Grateful 75
Moving On 76
Insanity 77
C.R.E.A.M. 78
Fall 80
Perception 81
A Letter From My Notebook 82
Clouds 83
Sorry 84
Pride 85
Hangover 86
Thinking Out Loud 87
Occupied 88
Perfect Strangers 89
A Poet's Confession 90
Grammar 101 pt. 3 91
Natural Causes 92
Blink 94
1%ers 95
Art 97

Objects In The Mirror 98
2:24 AM 99
Habits & Contradictions 100
Learning Backwards 101
Tap In 102
Smile 103
Awareness 104
Her Worth 105
Stunt Double 107
4:24 PM 108
The Single Song 109
Inspired 111
Know Yourself 112
10:01 PM 114
Note To Self 2 115
Nipsey Blue 116
Strangers 117
Flaws n' All 118
Ready 119

Note to Self.

Everything's gonna be okay
Even if it isn't right now
And the hill you're climbing
is more of a mountain
with every uphill step
a bit harder to take than the last.
And mistakes leave permanent scars
reminding us they're a sign of past pain,
and not that eventually you healed.
Even when you feel as if
you have every reason to believe
that things will never be the way
you see in the most vivid visions & dreams,
just breathe.
And remember that you've survived 100%
of what you been through,
And if you can keep going,
everything's gonna be okay,
it always is in the end.

Creator.

I wanna be everything
that they said you couldn't find.
And not to say I'll be perfect
but knowing I'll constantly try.

They say that women came
from the rib of men,
but as a man that knows better
I'll worship you like the creator you are.

Excuses.

I was recently asked
What I thought my worst qualities were
Before I replied,
I smiled with a sigh
Because I knew this meant
I'd have to reexamine
all the parts of me
that I hated for others to see.
That awkward part of me,
that still doesn't know how to trust
due to childhood traumas and dad issues
that always made me feel
like if the man that made me
could abandon me without batting an eye
it would only be a matter of time
before you would follow suit.
No matter what I would do,
Eventually it wouldn't be good
enough for you, but instead of
letting you reach that conclusion
alone, I'd come to it for you.
Make an excuse about why I
can't continue to get close to you
and proceed to find a way
to no longer occupy the space
that you once reserved for me
And my excuse would be that
I'm no good for you,
there's someone more suitable
because I'm damaged goods,
and you deserve something, someone
as flawless as my idea of you.

Torn.

Torn between wanting everything
in my life to be picture perfect,
while sacrificing inspiration,
and feeling the need to justify
why they can't be,
simply because I'm an artist
and I'm sensitive about my shit.

Self Love.

The only person
that I ever wanna love
more than you,
is myself.
And hopefully,
you feel the same way..

Learning Curve pt. 2

I've learned to be more careful
with who I choose to introduce
to my love
because the only way I've
ever been able to love
is diving head first
with no thought of the risk
or consequence.
But landing flat on your face
in a puddle full of potential
that you thought was
the deepest of pools
has taught me now,
before I commit to jumping
ever again, to make sure
that the water is deep enough
for a safe landing.

Obligated.

As a black man
it's my job to learn the game
and pass it down to our children.
We can no longer use ignorance
as a crutch and continue
making black children
that grow into black adults
having to start at ground zero

We need knowledge first,
and then we need structure.
Then we need businesses
we need ownership
we need stocks and trusts,
we need life insurance
we need land
we need things that appreciate.

Because when we die,
we can't pass a degree
or a good job down to our seeds.
So we need to be more aware
of what we have to leave behind
or we'll raise a generation
that'll be left with the task
of building what we were supposed to

Law of Averages.

My motivation to avoid mediocrity
by all costs was enough for me to change,
and it wasn't until I merged into another lane
was I able to look over
and realize how much traffic
there was on the road to average

Self Care.

Call me crazy,

but for some reason I'd rather struggle through it by myself, than ease my burdens at the expense of somebody else.

Whether that's right or wrong, I'll let you decide but as for me, in certain ways it made me strong.

I've always handled things alone.

I stress alone and cry alone and worry about my own life alone,

and for some reason or another, I can never bring myself to commit these acts in the presence of another.

My shell becomes my residence when the winds outside become dangerous and chaos is evident,

but instead of ever seeking protection and shelter in another, I repeatedly choose to act as my own refuge.

At times it hurts to admit, but my comfort in my solitude wasn't formed out of choice but necessity,

in order to prevent anything or anyone from ever again getting the best of me.

I often found myself disappointed when I gave my trust and entrusted myself in others from an early age, and ever since I can remember I've been afraid.

And like any choice made, choosing to be this way never comes without a price to pay,

some of the side effects that proved to hold true include:

a nonchalant attitude that masks emotions potent enough to make it appear as if I never care,

distancing myself from family and friends for times that always extend and acting as if nobody else would care enough to be there anyway.

Hesitation to be vulnerable in certain situations that I'm facing, and a fake smile I flash from a mile away to keep conversations of my self-concern at bay.

I'd rather struggle through it by myself than make it easier at the expense of somebody else.

But I know we all need help,

it's not easy to allow yourself to openly receive something you've never felt.

So charge my imperfections to my mind instead of my heart because my intentions in the end are always meant to be well,

but before I let anybody else choose to help, I'll always choose first to try to help myself.

Listen.

It's crazy how the universe spoke to me,
when I finally started listening.

I heard voices I was ignoring
telling me exactly what to do
and revealing my next move
in the whisper of the wind.

I saw visions,
I thought were only dreams
and the path towards them
illuminated by the stars.

All of this had been there
well before I gave them the attention
they were deserving of
but once I did I could see why
they couldn't wait to show me
everything I was missing out on

Guilt Trip.

Ladies of the jury,

as I stand before you today I'd like to enter my plea as guilty.

Guilty to acting like I couldn't see the man you needed me to be.

For being the reason it never seemed to work, for getting you right where I wanted to and right as you seemed to step forward, I retract

Forcing feelings to backtrack, or leaving them right where they stopped at,

and making you carry on and act as if your heart was still perfectly intact,

I plead guilty to that.

I plead guilty to countless counts of spent amounts of time and energy over genuine conversation and drunken memories,

where for just that moment, we were in love.

I'm guilty of making you feel like you were the only woman that existed when we kicked it,

vibes too strong to leave denied left us both finding refuge in each other's brown eyes.

I'm guilty of kissing your lips with good intent, and touching you like my every breath depended on the feel of your skin,

even if I stayed alive for just that night.

Only to close myself off right before giving your heart the reciprocity that it needed to see, and then telling you that "it's not you, but me."

I'm guilty.

I'm guilty of having your heart in my hands and not knowing what to do with it, until my passive and distant ways made you feel like I was through with it.

One of the worst crimes a man can commit

A man afraid to acknowledge the mistakes of his past can never use them as lessons with another lover he may have,

but you can also never walk forward continuing to look back.

So all I ask from the jury today, is forgiveness for crimes committed under the influence of the immaturity of a man finding his way.

Forgive me for killing us with my own insecurities,

If you can find a way to possibly forgive me

I'll never taint the innocence of another for as long it takes to amend my mistakes.

If you can really forgive me, never again will I have to plea guilty.

Less is More.

When we think about a better life
it's always assumed
that the only way to improve
is through adding something new.

But what we rarely learn
is that it's not always about
bringing in more
but learning when to throw
some things away
and clear out some space

Betrayal's Interlude.

Not too many feelings feel the same as being betrayed,

and because of that reason, to ever trust another again I'm afraid.

I'm afraid because I was once fearless,

never scared of the possibility to give pure intentions and positive energy to everybody and everything,

never scared to love, to help,
or to give some of myself to a complete stranger in need.

But nobody ever told me that a knife in the back would be the reason I'd begin to bleed.

Not too many things hurt more than feeling as if you did it all right only to be left in the end with nothing,

when you can't help but wonder why you were the one hand picked to be the example,

even when what you felt what you did on your end was ample.

But in this world it seems like the ones that give the most end up with the least to show,

the ones that water the seeds of others are the ones left struggling to grow.

So much so to the point I no longer look to the sky and ask why,

why the tears I cried weren't meant to come down another set of eyes.

Why every time I want to do nothing but right, failure and destruction ride parallel in my blindside.

Maybe I was meant to suffer so my story could save another, but who's autobiography was meant to save me?

Who do I lean on in my own weak times of need besides me?

And why is finding these questions unanswered continuously the only consistent tendency?

But for some reason my heart refuses to turn completely cold anyway, even when I feel I have every reason to be.

Even when I feel I have every reason to hate, every reason to blame,

every reason to see that same stranger in need and now look the other way.

My soul can't help but love harder despite how many times it was left abandoned and wanted to wither away,

I can't help but to continue to give of me fearlessly even if in the beginning I love slow and afraid.

No matter if giving until nothing is left is the toll I was meant to pay

my heart still yearns to love, even after it's been betrayed.

The Key.

The ones that end up being great
are the ones that find a way
to outgrow their insecurities.
At some point,
what you think about you
has to matter more than
what they think about you.
Even if you're the only one
that thinks it.
But the key is to be so secure
in your self-conviction
that over time,
you make everyone around you
believe it too.

INNERGY

**IF YOU DON'T TRAIN THE MIND
TO LISTEN TO THE SOUL,
YOU'LL FIND YOURSELF LOSING
TO YOUR OWN EGO EVERY TIME**

This is Americkkka

We live in a country
where black women and girls
are disappearing on their way
from school and work.
Black men and boys
are used as bullseyes
and the ones that hit it
get an all-expenses paid vacation,
and some still have the audacity
to ask me why I'm so passionate
about the protection of my people.

Footage of A Fallen People.

I wish I could've walked home with Trayvon Martin that day,

I wish Sandra Bland would've let me ride shotgun

I wish I could've ran out that store with Mike Brown so he didn't have to figure out a few dollars is how much they thought his life was worth...

I wish I could've played at that park with Tamir Rice because who knew that being a kid wrapped in melanin made you perfect target practice

I wish I was standing with Eric Gardner outside that store, the thoughts of hearing "I can't breathe" still leaves my own chest empty of air waiting for my next breath that he was never able to take

I wish Freddie Gray chose to stay home that day,

I wish Jonathan Ferrell didn't have car trouble, I wish Alton Sterling would've ran out of CDs right before 4 shots to the chest would be his calling card to eternal rest

I wish I would've went to Walmart with John Crawford, he went from grocery shopping to his family shopping for caskets in a matter of hours

Walter Scott, Kendrec McDade, Sean Bell, hell if you have time to listen I have names for days

And I'm tired.

I'm tired of black families forced to live without a father, a mother, a son, daughter, or damnit just someone that meant a lot to them

I'm tired of our beautiful black mothers, wives, sisters, and daughters forced to pick up the pieces and rule their once shared kingdoms in solitude,

Handling watching your kings get slain like peasants in the street and yet you hold your head high and handle it so gracefully you beautiful queens you ...

Soul Notes

I'm tired of kids forced to fill bloody footsteps left by fathers killed in broad daylight in HD, yet ironically racial ignorance has always served as the best blinders

Confirmation of a broken nation is as clear as the endless camera footage stained with unarmed black blood,

even if we say "don't shoot" and have proof as to why you never needed to, they refuse to see truth...

even if it's caught on tape.

So I ask you,

how long do you have to be patient before you're allowed to become impatient?

How long do we wait?

How long do we stay deep rooted and watch our people attempt to bloom in a place that loves everything about us except for...us

How long will we be that rose growing from the concrete?

Battered, bruised, and a few petals missing here and there yet...still growing, still standing

As I wipe the last tears from sleepless eyes and attempt to put my mind and this pen to rest, I pray for my people.

Because I know they're tired too,

I don't want anymore beautiful black souls turned into hashtags.

Love Drunk.

Being love drunk is real.
Where you're so infatuated
It's mentally intoxicating.
Decision making becomes impaired
and vision is compromised,
thoughts and words are slurred
and memories forgotten
as we can no longer recall
how we even got to this point.
We wake up to a still spinning room,
migraines and body aches
unaware of our actions
no matter how regretful.
And that's the price often paid
When we choose to love
certain people and things
that may not be
the best for us.

Drink responsibly.

Grammar 101

Your...
Is that **yours**?
All that time wasted on **your** doubts?
You might wanna listen to **your** heart because one day all those moments that you thought were all **yours** to procrastinate with will soon be **your** deadline.
Live **your** life now. It's **yours** to waste.

You're...
You're perfect.
You're worth it...all of it
The faster you understand *you're* meant to be the things you aspire to be and *you're* already the owner of that key to life that you search for so desperately...
The sooner *you're* able to find peace
You're the director of **your** movie

Manifest.

My power to manifest
thoughts and words
has been my biggest gift
and at times my worst curse

Some of my best feats
as well as biggest downfalls
have all had their birth
in what I gave life to
with my thoughts and words.

All in.

Once I know you're really down,
There's never a height
That I'm unwilling to climb to,
a sea I won't swim across
a road I won't travel down
a problem I refuse to solve
a bridge I think twice about building
or a war I refuse to fight,
in order to show you
that since you trust me,
I'm willing to risk it all
and go through whatever
to show you I got you.

Inaudible.

I have a hard time
believing that a God
is sitting there watching
as the world becomes corrupt
and our Earth is demolished
our children die
our women abused
our men imprisoned,
and in all his glory
and omnipotence
able to make it all better
with one spoken word
yet chooses to remain speechless

The Great Compromise.

I'm in this space,

where I don't know whether to pull you closer or watch you walk away.

And I know you're probably tired,

I let you take one step closer only for me to take two back as feelings seem to retract faster than they appeared.

Everything we do is on my time and before I leave myself comprised my pride never seems to want to peacefully resign,

and I'm stuck between thinking maybe we were meant to be, or maybe I'm just crazy.

Stuck between scared of losing us, but even more afraid of not finding myself first.

And at this point all I'll ever ask for is patience.

Give me time to grow through growing pains and balance momentary losses combined with temporary gains,

let me figure out my route.

Sometimes I just feel like I was meant to be the lesson,

meant to be the reason that after me you'd know to be done with second guessing.

And maybe you were meant to take the journey by my side,

or maybe just to temporarily steer me straight before you see me on my way.

Stuck not knowing how many chapters of my life will feature your name, or if it's meant to see its end on this page

I'll never expect you to wait forever because I'm eager to see potential turn into promise just like you,

knowing that you're the definition of treasure but your worth will always be compromised in the eyes of a fool.

But until my life's puzzle takes shape all I can pray is that you choose to help me sift through the pieces,

But I couldn't be upset if you felt like I let you slip between cracks and creases and left your heart on hold never to hear from a recipient.

And when you leave, I know it'll be because you felt like I already made an exit mentally.

So I know I don't have the pleasure of taking forever in order to get my shit together,

But while I'm trying,

I'll do my best to leave your love uncompromised

Make Change.

If change happened overnight
we'd all wake up
as a different version of ourselves
whenever it was necessary.

But since it takes time
and a process that requires
sacrifice and compromise,
we all too often choose
to tell ourselves it's okay
to remain unchanged
while the best versions
of ourselves in most vivid dreams
remain just that

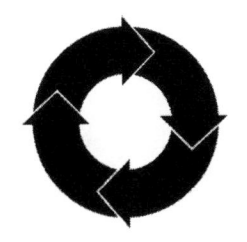

War Stories.

The heart is the same shape of a grenade,
that's why I could never
let you hold on for too long
because I'd never forgive myself
if I was your cause of death.
I'd much rather it be
that I'm the only causality
while I'm at war with myself.

Soul Notes

9:40 PM

I have detachment issues.
For as longs I could recall,
it's been difficult for me
to let anyone as close as
I really want them to be

I've mastered the ability
to immediately take the
closest exit at the mere
thought of being with someone
that was actually capable of
loving me with the patience
that I required and desired
to show me that she had
absolutely no intentions of flinching
no intentions of switching
since she knew she'd unlock
a love deep enough
for her to drown twice in,
and what was residing behind
this wall I spent my whole life
laying brick by brick
was well worth every second
she spent knocking it down
because what she found
was a man willing and able
to put his woman
on a pedestal so high
the constellations had competition.

But sadly I was even better
at doubting the mirror
and convincing myself that
she deserved better,
and I deserved worse.
To me she was perfect
and there was no way
she'd want to deal with me,
so instead
I detach myself

Call Casting.

Every movie doesn't deserve a sequel
and very few have a good one.
So if our love ever runs its course
to the point we decide to give it up
the last thing you'll ever have
to worry about is me trying to replay
a lead role in your life
when we were now meant
to audition for different parts

9:21 AM

One of the worst habits
we all have from time to time
is living our lives
through the perception in others' minds

Grammar 101 pt. 2

There...
There will be days when you wish **there** were just a few more hours in the day, days *there* will be perfect weather
There will be days where you have to go *there*...
to that place deep in your heart, your soul, the depths of yourself just to make it to bed that night
There will be rain, but *there* will always be another sunrise too.

~~Their~~.
Own that shit.
~~Their~~ opinions don't matter because they couldn't handle all you've endured on ~~their~~ best day
Stay away from people who spend ~~their~~ time being ~~their~~ own demise, sewing ~~their~~ seeds of bad energy unaware that they won't be happy with ~~their~~ results when it's time to harvest
Don't let ~~their~~ karma be yours too.

They're.
They're the people you care about,
they're your family and friends,
they're people you don't even know that secretly kept you afloat because they're praying for you.
They're that random stranger that helped you out for no reason
The one that gave you a genuine compliment out of the way.
They're the reason I think love still exists in the world
As long as *there* is good in ~~their~~ hearts they're bound to leave the world a better place.
Make sure they're the people you keep the closest.

Disconnect.

I've learned
that sometimes
one of the best ways
to recharge,
is to unplug.

Insomniac.
Low lights have always been
when I do my brightest thinking.
When it feels like the world is sleep
is when I feel most alive.
Quiet times always felt
like the best times for my soul
to yell loudest.

Picture Perfect.

You choose love, it doesn't choose you
when you meet someone
the feelings you begin to form
are a product of what you allow
yourself to see in them.
You choose to see that person as art,
no matter what others would consider
imperfect or incomplete
and make the decision that no matter
how abstract they may seem to appear
in the eyes of anyone else,
to you they're a masterpiece.

Sensitive.

Keep in mind again
that I'm an artist
and I'm sensitive about my shit.
But the crazy part is,
I can't take this advice and
not be my art's biggest enemy
and worst critic.
So many words written
that the world will never see
because of doubt and insecurity

#2

Recently I switched over
to writing all of my poems in pencil
in order to remind myself
that making mistakes was still okay,
and things in my life
could only be as permanent
as I make them.

Genesis 1:29

Nature is the only real
medicine that we need.
There will never be a pill
that can heal your soul
the same way sunshine will.
Supplements will never supplement
what we get from water and trees
no magic shake or tea
will ever truly heal you internally

Everything we really need,
was given to us for free.

Needs.

Hold my hand a lot.
Walk with me outside.
Kiss me for nothing all the time.
Joke with me.
Dramatically impersonate my personality.
Send me songs you'd think I love.
Go out with me and dance
like it's just us.
Ask me questions
that move me to provoke thoughts.
Cook with me to our favorite albums.
Take turns with me planning random dates.
Travel with me to every continent,
take a picture with me in every state
Tell me what I mean to you,
and be patient with me
on the days I'm a little harder to love.

OCD.

If it's not with all of you
love none of me,
and I'll do the same.

Comfort.

I abandoned my comfort zone
to make you happy,
only to notice that when
it came to me,
and the things I told you
that I'd need
you stayed in yours comfortably.

'16 Pessimist.

Maybe I was put here to break your heart....

You know, where a man meets a woman and they get consumed with a mutual passion that's too hot to even reside in hell.

And then like clockwork that same flame always dies...

Leaving us in that same dark space that we once occupied alone before we came into each other's lives,
searching for the first glimpse of light in another's eyes...

now that fire is just ashes of what used to be, ashes of memories, ashes of the potential we used to see...
and maybe I'm tormented the most because I know the reason it flamed out is because of me

Maybe I was just meant to be the lesson, like a professor I break down all your inhibitions in the syllabus of your heart...and that's where we start:

Chapter 1: You have my attention,
Chapter 2: Learning you and all the things you mention
Chapter 3: I could see a reality that featured we, but let me not admit too soon that you might have the key to me

A quick pop quiz is next....and you passed that test with flying colors...
when I finally make you climax so high you're looking down on mountains like ant hills,

as you spill your passion on my sheets and I explore your body with my tongue to the greatest of lengths until I find that destination that makes you speak my name on repeat like a like a broken record....but back to the lesson

Chapters 5, 6, and 7 fly by....as we sit there taking notes wondering if jumping off that bridge of commitment with your hand in mine is worth a try, filtering through lies and exposing flaws to one another that would surely mean our demise if witnessed by another pair of eyes…. This shit is getting crazy

And then comes that damn chapter 8….
this is the one I hate,

because right before I let you near, become transparent enough for you to peer through me as if I'm crystal clear, I disappear.

Because deep down I know I'm no good for you,
and as you continually push for me to pull things through, I dress in all black because I know this will only lead to us attending your hearts funeral.

Because maybe I'm not the one for you… and these skeletons that I've piled up and collected of love left unresurrected is the proof

Maybe I'm not the one for anybody…
maybe that's why I've always enjoyed my own company more than most, maybe that's why my heart refuses to be the host of this sitcom of love.

Maybe everyone doesn't have a soulmate or maybe I'm just the odd number left out that God decided to stop on leaving me without a match.

Maybe you're the patch….
but the problem is now a few stitches can't fix this broken heart of mine,

I need full out surgery, complete with a nose job and a face lift because this heart right here, I barely recognize this shit

Maybe it's so fragile, so protected that it's too dangerous to share..
and maybe at this point in my life I no longer care.

Maybe I'll be alone forever, but maybe…just maybe,
that might be for the better

Weight.

At least we can say we tried,
even if "we" eventually turned back
into you and me.
But we did try.
We tried to save each other,
before we first saved ourselves
and ended up drowning
in love's lake,
not because of each other,
but because of our own weight.

Reassure.

I like reassurance.
Tell me that I'm doing it right.
Tell me that I still have you.
Tell me that even when we fight,
you won't leave because no disagreement
is worth giving us away.
Tell me that you're here to stay.
Tell me why you love me,
at the most random times.
Tell me that you still have a thing for me,
that our moments of intimacy
are still your favorite daydreams.
Tell me that when I hold you
our heartbeats still begin to synchronize.
I need to know I'm still your security.
It feels good to hear,
that I'm still your safe haven .
And I need to hear these things from you,
not constantly but time to time.
And you have my word,
that I'll do the same
so you'll never be left
swimming in uncertain waters
when to keep you out of harm's way
all I have to do,
is reassure you.

Baggage Claim.

Everybody comes with something,
and usually that comes with adjusting.
But what I've grown to learn
is that it's usually not the baggage
that will push someone away
but whether or not that other person
is worth helping carry some of the weight with.

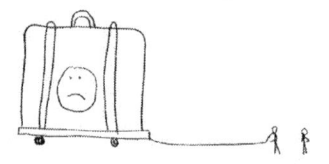

Integration.

I'll guess I'll be the one to say it,
but it seems we were better off segregated.
Not to say that you have to hate another race,
but any time we were left to build the reality of our own black lives,
we thrived.
Integration did nothing but take black talent and black dollars away from us,
and hand it on a silver platter
to the same people we have to convince that black lives matter.
I've seen no pictures of white children being harassed on their way to school
to sit in an all-black classroom.
No other people were arrested
for sitting at the counter of a black restaurant.
Nobody else had their most successful communities raided & bombed.
The entire world mimics everything we do from music to culture,
and loves to imitate and participate,
and wear everything we create,
except our oppression and unwarranted hate.
But whenever we've been left alone,
and had space to let our own magic operate,
we always made a way.

Understanding.

Before you ever attempt to love me,
first get me.
Learn how I love
and how I wanna be loved back.
Learn my trauma,
so that you know my triggers.
And before I allow you
sole possession,
give me the freedom
to first own myself.

Redemption.

For some strange reason, I have a feeling that redemption of what we shared has been on your mind lately

Even though we both know that a few roads are better off left untraveled upon twice...

and sometimes this round trip of love we thought we booked together with a destination to forever and back turns into a one way ticket

Redemption seems synonymous with re-commitment but I think I'm no longer in a position to deal with commitment to something that has seen the peak of its potential already...

So asking all those stars to realign back into the exact position of our love's constellation to duplicate a sky identical to the night I met you is a tall order.

It's hard for me to figure out where we'd even start again if we had to..

I think it's because I saw the writing on the wall and if you're reading this right now it's too late

I listened when they said two wrongs will never make a right so I think it just might be best not to answer the question of what is left between our souls incorrect twice.

Mainly because the cost of failed redemption is always a hell of a price,

but this joint account of our hearts now lies in the negative even though at one point so much was so willingly deposited by us both.

We don't need to redeem that energy, because if it's just not just right, right now, it will never be.

Maybe those once sweet heavenly melodies that rang out at full blast from our hearts' speakers doesn't need to be echoed twice.

Maybe another jump start to our passion's battery isn't necessary after all and it's better off left dead anyway

And I learned when something's dead there's a reason we bury it in the first place.

The irony is that long after thoughts of redemption disappeared from my mind you've been busy at work trying to redeem "we," redeem the things that used to be, but now I think I'd much rather spend time trying to redeem myself from you...

So as I balance myself on the remains of this wobbly step stool that was once an endless ladder of love, I hope to redeem those things on that very top shelf we deemed to be out of reach forever,

and maybe if I reach just a little harder, stretch my arm a little farther, I can watch all those precious artifacts filled with the nostalgia that we created together plummet towards the ground and shatter like they never even mattered,

But as I feel around for any remaining retrospect left behind I realize that nothing was there to begin with, that in order for us to be at a point of redemption something had to be missing.

A second chance is always a noble thought,

thinking we can blot away at those dirty stains we put on this once pure linen we shared in the beginning, but no amount of redemption can ever erase such a permanent blemish...

It reminds me of holding on to a balloon

and no matter how much of me wants to keep that string of your heart in my hand so that you belong to me and me only, there's a reason that the moment I loosen my grip on you it's your natural instinct to fly away...and I'll never be the reason you don't ascend...

even if it's alone.

Let my redeem my mind, you've lived there long enough...

redeem that piece of me I can never give to another because it's been held captive by you for far too long, and damn your grip is strong

But I have to redeem everything I need to move on.

And before I let go if I could please redeem one thing....let me redeem the memories...
because I think they'll be better off in the place I decide to set them free,

it'll be a place far away from both of us...

and to be honest with you I think that might be best.

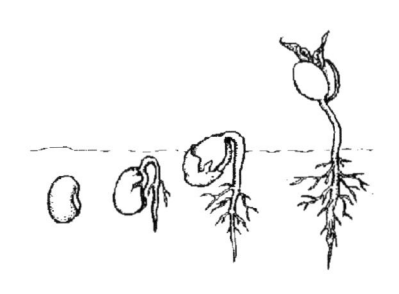

Still.

I still have some healing to do,
some lessons I've yet to learn.
And as uncomfortable as it is,
until I allow myself time to grow
I'll never be able
to say that I ever blossomed
into the version of myself
that I imagined in my head.

Ironic.

For all the days
that my pen was paralyzed
and I couldn't move myself to words,
those always seemed
to be the exact same days
that my mind felt as if
there was the most to say.

11:49 PM.

I do a lot of things alone
but I'm rarely lonely.
I taught my soul
how to embrace itself
when no other arms are available.
I taught my voice
how to speak life into my own ears
instead of repeating doubts and fears.
I taught my hands
how to clap for myself
when I'm the only audience.
I taught my feet
how to follow their own path
even if it's one untraveled.

Need Me.

A want is something you desire deeply
but can live without.
A need is something that without it
you wouldn't be able to live normally.
Now please understand this,
I want you.
I wanna put you on a pedestal
so high heaven had something
to look up to.
I wanna touch you every time
like I'll never feel your skin again.
I wanna kiss you
like my lips were custom fit
for every inch of your soul.
I wanna make love to you
in a way that makes a silent room
echo 90s R&B off the walls.
I wanna protect you in a way
that made you feel you always
had a lifeline in any situation.
I wanna do all of this
because I want you,
and that I'm unafraid to admit.
But please never forget
that as bad as I want you
I don't need you.
And the only one I'll ever really need
is me.

Unattainable.

We live in a world
where they make us want it all,
and then make sure most of us
can never afford it.

Up.

The ups took me higher
than the downs ever pulled us,
and for me that's all I need
to feel like it's worth it.
At the end of the day,
all I wanna know
is that the valleys
that we stumble upon
pale in comparison
to the mountaintops
that we'll reach together.

Red Pill.

No matter how it all goes down
at the end of the day
your reaction to
everything you go through
will always be on you

Friend Zone.

I'm tryna get in your friend zone,

I know we think we can skip it and still build solid commitment but,

before I can be anything close, your friend is something I need to be most.

I'm tryna do it the right way so if things get rough you'll have good enough reason to wanna stay on those days.

Our friend zone has to be our safe place,

I want our friend zone to be our mend zone, the place that we build on,

I wanna share our lives' stories and talk about all the things with old lovers that went wrong.

I wanna discuss fears and what makes us switch gears and the things capable of bringing us both tears.

I don't wanna rush the sex and the extra affection that comes next,

because if we start down this road too soon our friend zone won't be a comfortable room.

And if I think I'm here to complete you like I claim I'm capable, I need to see what's inside you before I get inside of you

I need to stroke your mind before stroking what's between thighs comes into play,

and I want our mental foreplay to last all day,

until we both know our way to each other's inhibitions so well it'll be impossible to stray.

I need to know you and not just about you,

I need to know where your confidence resides and what makes you doubtful.

I need to know you so well that your story becomes like a book too easily read,

Our comfort should be so real that we can sit and not share a single spoken word and still know the deal,

But I wasn't always this way,

I made my own share of mistakes thinking that if we rush it wouldn't matter anyway and we'd figure it out along the way,

and that led to feelings before friends and all it did in the end is complicate.

But through the times I did it wrong each one taught me a lesson, so hopefully through learning my last is my next.

Most importantly I now know that I can't really have you unless I know you, unless we know each other

So before I skip steps and make mistakes again,

let's just start as friends.

A Virtue.

Always be patient,
but never overstay your welcome
in whatever situation
that's keeping you waiting.

Twisted.

They say when a heart breaks
it never breaks even.
So I guess that explains why mine
felt so out of shape
after you.
I felt like I gave you all of mine
while all I got in return
was the smallest part of yours
that you had left to spare.
So when you left,
you walked out with more
than you came with
while my chest was left
standing empty-handed.

Domestic Terrorists.

Muslims ain't knock down those towers, "Americans" did.
But it raised our kids to believe every person with a turban on must be a terrorist

I've never seen a poppy seed field in the hood, yet the hood has crack in every crevice.

Fluoride filled water was used in concentration camps to keep minds dull and damp,

so what else would you expect them to do but bring it to you and let that same poison flow from our own toothpaste and taps.

Sounds to me like this country is its own terrorist.

Fear will always keep the oppressed controlled, so that's what they perpetuate everyday.

There's a reason why our worst influences are the most glorified,

a reason why every time you see a tv it's featuring a false reality

As long as the mind of sheep are feeble and weak,

They feed us what they want us to believe and think that life is,

but it isn't.

Balance

I'm most at peace when I allow myself balance.
When I accept that I'm light as well as darkness,
chaos as well as order,
fire as well as water

I'm most at peace,
when I allow myself to be unfinished,
as well as a masterpiece.

Bad Day.

You didn't have a bad day,
the day had a bad you.
So next time we want to blame
the result of the day
on anything else other than ourselves,
we should first ask
what version of us
did we give to the day?

50/50

Accountability is a two way street,
that most only travel down one way.
We expect so many things from the ones around us,
but of ourselves we seem never to have identical requirements

Take Time.

It's important to take the time
to love yourself.
Away from distractions,
away from people,
away from everything,
except for yourself.

Take the time to breathe
take the time to heal
take the time to forgive
take the time to rebalance.
Take the time to do everything
that you need
in order to love yourself
just a little bit more.

Love Too Fast

I fall in love way too fast.

And maybe that's the reason
my past looks like campfires
that once lit up the night,
and now all you see is the remains.
Ashes of the memories that burned out
And half lit logs
that signify why it always seems
to die in the end

I fall in love too fast

because it's impossible for me
to not find the best qualities
in every woman I meet
and place them on a pedestal so high
that their imperfections
won't find a ladder long enough
to stand a chance

because the idea of romance,
and the ability to make a woman
feel like the goddess she is
with every word, touch, and kiss,
is embedded into me.
Even if I'm smart enough to know
that I should probably slow down.

Stay Woke.

If I could, I'd take the word "woke" on a trip in the biggest boat I could find to the middle of the deepest ocean and throw that shit away

Why can't taking the time to unlearn the lie our ancestors had beat into them, from white mediocrity to false religion, be the norm for all the people that look like me?

And I'm forced to be the one that stands out and sounds crazy because I don't believe what they feed me through the tv?

I'm weird because I see the plot,

how all of our streets are patterned liquor store, pawn shop, liquor store, a convenience store inconveniently owned by nobody that looks anything like me, and another one right across the street

A McDonald's that's killing me while "I'm lovin' it," and a Burger King where they sell me the dream of "having it my way"

I've watched every president in my lifetime do absolutely nothing to help the very people that built this country, while everyone with a different nationality were handed the keys to their dreams,

but when I say I know votes don't bring hope, I'm acting "woke"

I watched a black man get killed in the middle of Walmart, a black kid get killed at his neighborhood park by the police,

They "found" Sadaam in a cave, Bin Laden in his secret hideaway, yet Pac, Biggie, and Nipsey can get murdered in cold blood in front of the world but still remain unsolved mysteries

I have to be labeled as believing in conspiracies

I watched the president call the moon from a house phone on national tv, I can't get a signal on certain parts of my apartment, but I have to be crazy for saying we never went into space,

I'm "woke" for wanting to think differently from the information they're giving me because it never added up mentally

Because I took the time to figure out what my people did before slavery, and saw how humanity took everything we had, gave it new names, faces, rules, and races.

But I'm "woke" because others around me never took that same time and probably won't.

So at this point, "woke" ain't nothing but code for common sense to me, and they always warned me it wasn't so common

But as long as I'm here don't worry, I'll continue to be the one that looks crazy, but I find comfort knowing that in reality, it's the other way around

IDK

I don't know who needs to hear this but...

You're worth more than what you're currently selling yourself for.

Let's Get Married.

I wanna get married for all the wrong reasons...

Like being able to sing in the car with you and we trade between lead and ad-lib support,

Like being able to get on your last nerve and then pick you up and kiss your tolerance for me back into you.

Like every time we go out to eat we both know never to get the same thing so we can share entrees forever

Like being able to unlock each other's inner child and go outside and dance in our yard together in the worst of weather

Like spending Saturdays in our pajamas while binge watching each other's soul in the bed as Netflix asks us if we're still there

Like traveling the world and using each other as passports and scrapbooks to tattoo conjoined memories on our separate souls

Like being able to go out and do weird shit like approach you at the bar like we've never met and I have to figure out a new way to make you fall in love all over again.

Like rushing home from work just for that first embrace and you being my happy hour after the longest days

Like being able to publicly act like a fool with you in the middle of Target just because your laugh makes me feel like answered prayers

Like telling you the truth to the point where the only thing that could ever feel false between us is dishonesty

Like being able to show you every hidden piece of me, and you're still not afraid of the view

Forgiveness.

I'll never quite understand
how I can be so forgiving
of the mistakes made by others,
but when it comes to mine
I have a tendency to carve my own
permanent in stone,
never to be forgotten.

Grateful.

I'm grateful.
Even when I feel ungrateful.
Even when all my focus is on
my self-subscribed shortcomings.
Even when I feel as if my Marathon
has been all uphill and I see
everybody else around me
running Victory Laps.
I take a step back and notice
that I had the portrait out of focus
because I only zoomed in
on solely the imperfections
but looking at the bigger picture
put all the flaws into perfect perception.
They were meant to be there
because a masterpiece never
called for or required perfection.
And when you do decide to refocus
you'll notice how much you have
that you ignore on a daily basis,
others would love to trade places
Just to show you it could always be worse
Just to show you how many things
you owe a world of gratitude to.
So for the rest of forever
take some time out your day
to just be grateful.

Moving On.

I've never been with someone twice, and I've never even tried.
An ex never got a chance to again be the next,
because I'm a firm believer that if we were really meant to be
that's something you recognize the first time.
I feel like if it's meant to be permanently,
when things aren't ideal like they will sometimes be,
we fight with everything we have
and hold on by every single thread
exhausting every option possible before we choose to give up.
We'd rather figure it out before we even think of going separate ways,
and our worst nightmare would be you seeing your dreams
in the eyes of someone other than me.
And watching something we once thought was meant to be,
turn into temporary.

So if we ever decide to let it go,
just know you'll never have to worry about me
wanting second chances.

Insanity.

Read something the other day that said
"Poetry teeters on the edge of insanity"

And that's the closest answer I've ever heard
for the reason I've felt crazy my whole life.

C.R.E.A.M.

I hate money.

I hate money because we all love money.

First I hate money because it's fake,

literally defining the value of our lives by how many pieces of paper we collect

Never realizing that debt is the leading cause of stress and stress is the leading cause of death

I hate money because it stole our true purpose

We're the only living things on this earth that aren't doing the things we were truly born to do..

trees grow freely and birds fly wherever life takes them

Fish explore the depths of the ocean, even us as children unshaped by finances live our lives to the fullest potential

And then we grow up...

waking up daily after hitting snooze a few times to do something you're not in love with is the definition of insanity

Somehow we've managed to put a price on how much an hour of our time that we'll never get back is worth

Hoping for happiness to find us while we waste our lives away at a job,

I don't think our time was ever meant to be on a salary, I don't think life was meant to be lived with a snooze button

We really traded in our dreams for money...I guess we're all crazy

I hate money because it controls us,

dictating to us who matters and who doesn't even though wealth to me was always meant to be what you possessed internally

Fleets of people forced to sleep on the streets while others sleep in mansions with so many rooms they've only been in them once

Not knowing that that person walking on bare feet in the ghetto with nothing to eat could be the next great mind in humanity

But since he can't afford a way out surrounded by the clouds of past generations that lived the same life before him, please excuse him for being misguided

I hate money because it creates life cycles

It created war, it created guns, hate, envy, drugs, prostitution, greed, dead end jobs, routines, pollution, deception, broken families, the facade of chains and nice whips, minds filled with nothing but C.R.E.A.M,

people no longer think and the countless homes filled with all of it right now as we speak

I hate money because somewhere along the way it replaced our happiness,

and I don't think happiness was ever meant to come with a price tag.

I hate money,

Because without it we'd all be rich.

Fall.

I seem to change with the seasons,
and fall was always my favorite.
The reason it resonated,
is because summer flames die
and we really get to see
which ones were worth lasting into winter.
Even trees show us their true colors.
As everything around me,
seems to settle down,
I spring alive,
even as things around me
temporarily die.
But things meant to sustain,
always find a way
to make it through the fall.

Perception.

How we think the world perceives us,
is really the mirror
showing us how we perceive ourselves.

A Letter From My Notebook.

She told me to not to call on her again until I was ready to make her a commitment instead of a convenience

She told me that she was tired of being there every time I needed a shoulder to cry on in the form of a blank page, but always seemed to miss out on the stories that made my heart smile

She said she no longer wanted to be a punching bag that I beat down with sad soliloquies and things in this world that troubled me,

instead would rather be my pillow that put my pounding heart to ease and rocked me to sleep with the melodies I made with her strings playing perfectly in the background

And she was capable of that plus more because in her eyes typing my life on a screen could never love me more than she could when I let the words bleed from my pen into her lap

She said she was tired of being the mistress that I crept with on sleepless nights and random weekends, the plan B that never got to be put into act long enough for plan A potential

She never wanted to be the paul bearer in my life's funerals but instead the flower girl in all the weddings my soul turned into poems

If I let her She could be everything I needed her to be, but I never gave her a chance to prove herself to me

Clouds

The clouds never stay in one place.
No matter what storms or darkness some of them contain,
eventually they all move along.

Sorry.

I forgive you...
Now I know you think I'm disappointed in you and those are words you thought you'd never hear me say, but I get it....
and I forgive you

I forgive you for doubting yourself, smothering the light you have inside ashamed that if you let 'em see the real you they wouldn't approve

Because I know you saw the same thing happen to so many others by those who persecute with nothing to lose...
and for that I forgive you

I forgive you for the many fuck ups and the time wasted, and though hindsight is always 20/20 and that same precious time you bought is nonrefundable, that I understand...

and I forgive you

I forgive you because I know sometimes on those back roads of life the headlights are nowhere to be found and you can't lift your foot of the gas...

left to hold the steering wheel praying for guidance before another casualty happens and you collide head on with failure and disappointment yet again...

and I know that's something you never wanted, because the whole time I know it was dark outside....
and I forgive you

I forgive you because I lived with you, hell I lived in you...when you cried I cried when you lost so did I

When you were filled up with pride to the point where you were too heavy be to put aside I was there unmoved too. With every rise and fall, I too ascended and fell.

I forgive you because I am you,
and to forgive yourself is to forgive others too

Pride.

Pride comes before the fall,
or at least that's what they say
So does that mean,
That when I do fall
It'll at least serve as a cushion
for letting it get away?

But on second thought, I've learned
that it's best not to chance it
And always try my best to make sure
my pride isn't the reason
I ever find myself falling again.

Hangover.

They always said that drunken words were sober thoughts,
there may be some truth to that because that liquid courage is one hell of a drug

Blurring every line between lust and love until you can no longer tell them apart,
every shot you take to the head is also a shot you take to the heart

And you reload that gun time and again
Every bullet in that bottle you fire straight back until the room spins

Before you know it you're back in that same position you were in,
when you made that vow to yourself last time that you'd never get this drunk again

But you love how it makes time feel nonexistent, no past or future in sight
Only that faded present moment with nothing left for you to do except own it
Mixing brown and white better than desegregation while making that silent declaration on pacing,
but before you know it you've reached that familiar destination of intoxication

Drunk in love, drunk in hate, drunk in regrets and mistakes
Throw my phone in the nearest lake before it's too late

Hide it before I spill my drunken passion into a call or text that shouldn't be made,

Replaying memories that shouldn't be played
and then you wake up in the morning laying where you shouldn't have laid

Hungover not from the whiskey & tequila,
but hungover from the actions that each one of them featured

Thinking Out Loud.

Sometimes I wish I could think out loud
So you'd know how I felt without apprehension

I know you constantly wonder what's on my mind
About all the thoughts I fail to mention

On the outside I'm reserved, choosing to listen more than speak
But internally there's a war with thoughts that run deep

From reflection to introspection, even fears of regression
And just when my logic chooses words they lose direction

It's a gift and a curse to have the gift to observe
To see things for what they are and people for what they're worth

And the curse lies in when you can't put it into words

Sharing the contents of your mind tends to come with vulnerability
And potentially you fall subject to rejection and hostility

So for now I'll just think, I promise words eventually
But all the while just know, my conscience is speaking mentally

Occupied.

The only occupation that I desire to have,
is one that won't leave the world quite the same,

one that can only be done by me in such a way, that others
stumble clumsily when they try to fill my shoes

I don't want a job, where if I'm ever to be replaced,
it's just business as usual the next day.

Perfect Strangers.

You know me completely, yet you don't know me at all
Can tell me how I lived life, every rise every fall
You know my deepest secrets, stuff the world never knew
It's sad you know me so well yet I barely know you

You were there when I had nothing, just a prayer and a dream
And even when I had it all, at least that's just how it seemed
When I was lost without cause, you were the voice in my ear
And when I finally found a path, you walked beside with no fear

You helped me right all my wrongs, when I would trip and fall short
And put my life in perspective, when I felt out of sorts
When I need you the most, you tend to always be there
But sometimes when I seek help, you vanish into thin air

You make me feel like I can have it all, just try harder
You make me feel like a lost cause, and why even bother
I try to know you like you know me, before I'm too old
But it's not easy when the perfect stranger's your very own soul

A Poet's Confession.

A lot of my old poems began with me asking questions, that's something I noticed flipping back through these pages reminiscing…

Reminiscing on how at one point I didn't know that I would use this pen and my mind to harmonize like the perfect hook over a tight beat,

Reminiscing on how I felt like I had to do it like everybody else in order for it to be done right,

but it wasn't until I replaced those questions with confessions, those rhythmic rhymes with the offbeat rhythm of life's lessons that it wasn't gonna be…real

Life was never meant to rhyme all the time anyway

I tried so hard to write everybody's story except for my own when all along an autobiography was well overdue,

But as I Courage the Cowardly Dogged my way through a few more poems filled with half-truths leaving the most important lines unwritten and the necessary things to say unsaid, something happened

I had a meeting on the executive floor with my purpose and it told me that until you own your thoughts completely you'll always be a slave to your own conscience

Until you tell your story your book will always be unfinished, until you put your heart into your poems they will always be dead no matter how healthy the body of your words appears to be

I made a promise to my purpose, that every time I put ink to paper, I'd tell the truth

Grammar 101 pt. 3.

To
To really know the beauty of love you had **to** feel the pain of rejection

In order **to** grow you have **to** spend time in the ground,

you have **to** be dumb and naive in life at times in order **to** be wise in the end,

to complete something you first have **to** have the courage **to** begin

That's the hardest part.

Too...
Love **too** much,

laugh **too** much,

give **too** many hugs and kisses **to** people that deserve them,

spend **too** much time reminiscing with old friends about old memories when you run in*to* one another

Be **too** genuine, even when it may feel better

Doing these things will not only bring with it a life full of joy, and not only for them but for you **too**

But most of all, always love as if you were blind, it's never **too** late to be better

Natural Causes.

I despise 9-5s, so I figured I'd try writing my way to a better life instead

See writing doesn't feel like a job...

at times it's much better, but at times writing can be way worse than that blissful ignorance of clocking in and out for a shift because I don't know about you but writing brings things out of me

It brings out the best of times and the worst of times,

like a Tale of Two Cities but see my life is somewhere right in the middle of that Charles Dickens book and that J Cole song

Stuck between showing my good and my evils, hoping you accept my strengths and flaws along with my rights and wrongs...

because writing that shit does something to me

At times I feel like it takes the soul out of my body and puts it on the dinner table of life for everybody to have a piece until there's nothing left but scraps,

Because I don't know about you but I can only write what's inside of me

If I haven't lived it, felt it, touched it, passed or failed it I don't feel compelled to let this ink leave this pen because somewhere in that process that pen becomes me and that ink turns into blood and I'm not ready to bleed out just yet,

maybe poets were never meant to die of natural causes anyway

Every piece that I write, every thought that I've ever given life with these words is like a piece of me leaving that I'll never be able to own as just my own ever again,

and maybe because when I write I share so much of myself that's the reason I'm bad at sharing everything else

Soul Notes

Keeping my most precious pieces of me at the bottom of my heart like the deepest abyss of the ocean and since the world is mostly water anyway good luck finding that shit

But every now and then a piece of it floats to the surface,

flowing with the current until it gets washed up on the shore and I have no choice but to write about it

And whether it's a piece of a memory, joy, depression, past lovers, or future fears is usually never up to me

I never get to decide which wound will be reopened or what words will be used as stitches because real writing rarely gives you the privilege of choice

It's just a feeling

I don't always get to decide which way my blood will decide to run in between these lines on this paper, all I can do is hope that when I'm done bleeding I'm not dead just yet

That means I still have blood left, my heart is still beating, somewhere deep in me there's another story, another line, another word to be written

I just hope I get it out in time,

because it's rare that you find a poet that dies of natural causes.

Blink.

If it was up to me, I would never blink again

Because missing things has become a tendency,

I don't wanna miss another moment with those that mean the most to me,

but every time I blink it seems to be something that happened in between that I'll

never get back.

Every time we laugh, is one less laugh we'll ever share together

And good days that we wanted to last forever,

are now yesterdays that we can only visit in our minds

1%ers

I've never seen a gun factory or a poppy seed field in the hood yet the hood is flooded with enough product to arrest 1 out of every 9 black men by age 20 wait too late, they do that now anyway..

And is it me, or does jail look like a big black family reunion more than anything?

They were never made to protect & serve US, they were made to control our ancestors and disrupt any black progression even by wrongfully arresting or pulling out a weapon and saying they acted out of protection

The reason they started building projects like skyscrapers were to fit more of us in them regardless of the tenant as long as it's another nigga in it···

They send you to schools with text books that are missing too many pages to be used and written by a group of people with mentalities that expired in 1922,

No Child Left Behind was just some extra help to rush our babies to the unemployment line or asking someone "would you like to make it a combo, if not that'll be $7.29,"

and they die thinking all they'd ever amount to was giving back change instead of being one

They tell you what you know isn't as important as how you look, and if you don't believe it tell me the last time you've seen a commercial about a new law or reading a book

They control the stations that play your favorite songs and keep you in front of a tv all week watching the false reality of a celebrity while you waste away mentally, and don't even know it..

But if we're dumb and misinformed, at least we'll look good doing it..

They give MLK a street in the worst part of every city along with a McDonald's and Burger King to kill us off internally,

and all he wanted was to not be labeled before you examined the package

Our country is backwards, killing off all those whose flag is a rainbow and those that came on a slave ship instead of the Mayflower

Until love's power is more powerful than the love we have for power, we'll never move forward.

And I'm tired of standing still..

Art.

Never date an artist,
Unless you want to end up as material.

Soul Notes

Objects In The Mirror.

Hypothetically…

Let's just imagine that I really was what everyone thought me to be,

and I took my own advice half as well as I seemed to give it.

Imagine that I really felt as gifted as my potential seemed to exhibit,

at all the right times in front of all the right people in all the right places it seems to shine bright

but behind closed doors doubt and insecurity act as perfect blackout curtains to my life's uncertainties

Imagine I told you that although you think of me as someone who has mastered the ability to wait patiently, impatience has always been one of my worst qualities

I hate waiting.

What if I told you that depression has been the constant baggage of my soul's road trip even though I manage to bring just enough joy along when our paths cross for you to never notice

What if someone known for having all the answers really knows nothing,

full of pure intentions but an internal vision of a manifestation of bad decisions

What if I told you that I was lost in purpose with enough bad vices to death grip my mind and distort the picture long enough for reality's mirage to run its course

Imagine that as well as I string words together my communication is almost nonexistent in hopes to keep everyone at distance,

even those that know to me they mean the most

What if the man in the mirror wasn't the one that you recognized,

who would I be to you then?

2:24 AM

If we don't inspire each other to be better separately,
then we shouldn't be together.

Habits & Contradictions.

I have a few bad habits, but you were my worst one.

And it never mattered how long it had been or what's happened since then, your presence remained an addiction not easily tamed

Like discovering our heaven existed on earth, we gifted each other a beautiful curse

And even when the chemistry combined with anatomy our experiment always concluded with the most perfect of disasters

Our essence intertwined was always so strong, so deep that imitation with any other was impossible

Eyes are gateways to souls and yours led me right to the front door of yours,

where I came face to face with your deepest inhibitions and knew exactly what to do with them

We couldn't hide behind facades of false perceptions and countless misconceptions made by so many others that we never thought twice about,

We couldn't help but see each other for exactly what we were, and it was perfect.

And searching for similar substance from others constantly leaves us both disappointed,

but never in the addiction to the feeling that we gave one another,

that was something that can't quite be described with words.

Soul Notes

Learning backwards.

In classrooms full of seldom used theories of mathematics, we graduate with degrees but never taught how to do our own taxes

We learn that history starts with Columbus sailing the ocean blue in 1492, but never seemed to be concerned about the people he really took America from

We never learn that Africa was the most advanced place in the world first, full of riches, harmony, and well being

But we always get depicted as unintelligent jungle dwellers but our natural compassion and lack of murderous weaponry was the main reason we were conquered by Europeans

Only teach about us as the oppressed but never seem to have chapters about the success & times we thrived even against every odd defied

We teach that Thanksgiving was a peaceful exchange, but never learned that Pilgrims depleted a nation of its very foundation after they deceived a people that welcomed them with warm embrace

On 4th of July we think independence was gained that we've really yet to see, and even worse you never heard a word in school about Juneteenth

And if in 1776 slavery had yet to be abolished, why did we ever think the Declaration of Independence was ever written to include us?

We think that Thomas Edison and Alexander Graham Bell invented all our tools, but we never learn about the enslaved geniuses like Lewis Latimer that they took those same inventions from to use

The Statue of Liberty was originally a black woman with shackles broken off her feet, but once it was sent it America they sent it back to France and told them to change everything

We think the equality came with the movement for civil rights, but the irony is that oppression today is still just as high

Every black leader that was capable of inspiring change was slain by the government or framed and put in chains

The Black Panthers are the reason you ate free breakfast, and were never a terrorist group but formed out of necessity to protect us

Lies our teachers told us shaped our minds, and most of them were taught just as wrong
But until we know our own lyrics we can never in America truly dance to our own song

Teach our kids better because it starts with the youth, but don't let lies our teachers told keep us living a false truth

Tap In.

Your passion,
Your soul's potential and purpose
has nothing to do with becoming
someone that you're not,
and everything to do with tapping in
to who you already were
the day you were born.
What you're searching for,
isn't outside of you
but already dwells within.
And it's waiting on you
to realize that.

Smile.

Moment of transparency:
I'm extremely self-conscious about my smile.
If you notice, every time I do it
like clockwork after a second
I look away or down,
hoping that whoever is around
wouldn't sense my insecurity
and instead of wearing my smile proud
like the brightest badge or crown,
I treat it like a permanent typo
that I hope the world reads over
without noticing.

But recently,
someone caught that first second,
right before I start second guessing
and told me that when I smiled,
really smiled without inhibition
or concern about who's around,
it was like my soul would light up
and everything in me came alive

So from now on, maybe I'll try
to not be so fast to hide my smile.

Awareness.

If I asked you
what color you thought the sky was,
you'd probably say blue,
and you'd be wrong.
It's black.
We see it as blue
when our sun illuminates
the area around it.
But when it disappears
we get to see the sky
for what it really is.

Keep that in mind,
next time you feel you have all the answers.
There is always a reality that exists
outside our circumference of awareness.

Her Worth.

She just wanted to know why.

Why wasn't she good enough to be the one to make him change, or why when she got closer he would back away?

She wanted to know why things weren't the same,

in the beginning it was blue skies and sunshine, but attempted progression proved to present clouds of doubt carrying rain.

She's no dummy, so when the text was left unread or even worse with no reply, she knew that's when she'd lost your mind.

And every time you hit her with that "I've just been busy" line, she remembered when you were just as busy but still managed to make time.

The communication is what first made it amazing,

when your words matched your actions and the art of conversation you created together was the most beautiful distraction

And she used to feel perfect when she was with you, but now her time feels borrowed and your vibes make her more insecure and confused

She said just let her know if she wasn't the only one,

and in the beginning she only asked you one thing and that was "please, just don't have me out here looking dumb."

All she wanted was clarity,

if it was just about the sex then tell her and let it be, but don't mislead her with false dreams depicting scenes and things you knew you could never really see.

She gave it all to you, and she felt like you took it and in return didn't leave her anything.

She wanted to love through all the mistakes, but once the trust breaks it's hard to replace something that was never meant to change.

And eventually, she got tired of feeling underappreciated and admired less, and decided that maybe moving on was best.

But before she left, she looked at you, but not with hate or regret,

but hurt because she felt her love was inferior, when she really gave you her best.

Stunt Double.

A vibe like mine
won't come around twice.
I don't care who you choose
to attempt to fill my shoes,
I don't care what man
you cast to act as my stunt double,
I don't care if they have more money
or more social clout,
I don't care who you meet,
they'll never quite be me.

And you know they won't,
because I treated your body
like a sanctuary on Sunday,
filled your mind with precious jewels,
and fed your soul like a flower
that I never wanted to see die.

So I always wish the best for you,
but we both know
even though I was far from perfect,
you knew I'd do anything
to learn how to love you perfectly.

4:24 PM

What a world…
where half of it is starving
and the other half is obese.
Where cops cause more fear
than they do a sense of security.
Where our alter egos live in our phones
and our shortcomings and failures
are never shown

The Single Song.

Being single is cool 'till ain't nobody around, and you wake up to a bed half empty and a room with no sound

No soft voice or that bliss from a good morning kiss or early morning laughter about something from last night,

I woke up, to nothing but the ghosts of other women sleeping by my side.

Being single is cool, until you have to pursue, and find that feeling from many women that the right one can give you.

But those episodes tend to end faster than TV syndicated shows, and that temporary feeling of completion is gone as soon as they put back on clothes,

being single is cool, 'till ain't nobody you can call your own.

I'm not saying we're all ready for relationships, and maybe this life journey hasn't taken me on all its necessary trips before I was meant to slip,

but I've fallen before, and when I needed to be held up the most, I ended up on the floor.

So instead of loving more I allowed myself to grow cold and even the score, vowing to never be vulnerable enough to let love last for more than one night and nothing more.

And eventually, all of my "let's just be friends," turned into friends that I don't have anymore.

Losing myself in friends with better benefits than government jobs, only to notice I'm not benefitting myself in the end at all.

Being single is cool, until one day you look around, and notice you've built nothing with another because you never allowed it a chance to leave the ground.

Being single is cool 'till ain't nobody left to love.

And one day my next will be my last and my present will be synonymous with the decisions made in my past.

One day after I'm done running I'll look back and realize nobody's near, because I kept you at a distance and never allowed you to see me perfectly clear,

and living a life without love is slowly turning into my biggest fear.

So being single is cool, until one day all your friends have to leave you because they have love at home to tend to,

and that feeling is something no other person can lend you, and even when torn by hurt the right love has always been the perfect stitches to mend you.

So before you wake up like me, take advantage and love back who's trying to love you currently.

Because me, I've probably used all my chances at failed romances.

And all because, I never allowed myself to be easier to love.

Inspired.

I've been really
inspired lately,
to turn my not yets into right nows
and confirm the rest of my maybes.

Know Yourself.

At times I feel like a walking contradiction,

It's funny I've been told that I was made to stand out but will always hate attention

Introverted in love with being alone, but a lover of all people and value relationships and memories made more than anything I own.

And I know,

I've never been best at communication on a regular basis,

but just know there's never a day your presence doesn't dance with my prayers.

I'm a materialistic minimalist.

I like nice shit,

but I know the happiness it brings is always only momentarily and it really won't matter in the end.

Battling between not caring about anything and buying things to feed the greed of my own subtle subconscious insecurities.

I love hard but I let go easily,

sometimes before I should and assume the worst before I attempt to give anybody my best.

And I continue to hide behind the same excuse saying any love ever meant to be kept will always remain effortless.

But in reality I use that to mask my fear of giving everything of me,

and it not being a good enough effort for us.

The best advice giver for everybody else, but the absolute worst at giving that same advice to myself.

Guiding others towards becoming their best selves, yet I'm only a shell of mine.

I know exactly what needs to be said and all the things you could ever expect next,

Yet....

I choose to feel my way along the wall of life's dark room finding out what lies usually by stumbling my way through.

All of my flaws are visible, from all the times I fell and came back to my feet scraped and bruised.

But for the moment hopefully they can be excused, while instead they're used to bring clarity to my own distorted views.

How do I live a life of helping others lacking the ability to help myself?

I'm at war with myself, from my constant contrasting of logic verses what I felt.

And for the first time in forever,

I'm facing my own reflection laying eyes on all my imperfections

But it was time,

because acknowledging exactly what's in the mirror and not what you want to be there,

has always been the best way to really know yourself.

10:01 PM.

Even if it doesn't work out,
and we both decide
that "us" isn't best for us
and your heart would rather
not be meant for me,
please remember one thing:
every word I said to you,
came from a pure place
and even though now
we may no longer feel that way,
at that point in time
it's exactly what I meant
with exactly that intent.
So don't feel that now,
because it didn't work out
that when I told you
that you had me
when I told you I cared
and my eyes didn't want
to be occupied by any other,
and my soul wasn't meant
to be elsewhere shared,
never think that I ever
told you things I didn't mean,
no matter if our romance
decided to impersonate a tragedy

Note To Self 2

Yesterday you said tomorrow.

Nipsey Blue.

The day Nip died,
I cried the rest of that night.
You would've thought he was family
the way the tears
found a way to race down my face,
but this hit so different
because I was in tune with his mission.

As a kid from the hood
that beat the odds before
he died and made it out,
and once he did, went back
to see who he could show the route.

He turned Crips into capital
and Bloods into businessmen
and used his voice and lyrics
to show us how to work the system.
And for the ones that listened
he dropped gems in his music,
told us to be royalty and owners
not just n***as and b****es.

I was too young to cry
when Pac died, but this had to be
exactly what it felt like.
His kids lost their brightest guiding light
his wife lost her main lifeline
the hood lost a leader
and the world lost a prophet.
At the hands of a system
that saw him paradigm shifting.

But what they didn't know
is that you can't destroy energy
and what they really did in the end
is give a lil' more Neighborhood
to the souls of you and me,
so with that same energy
and a Marathon left to continue
my favorite color from here on out,
is Nipsey Blue.

Strangers.

What if we had chosen
to just remain strangers,
and managed to keep our hearts
out of the potential danger
of never being as big again
if things between us
didn't seem to pan out
and we were both left
with bloody hands?

Flaws n' all.

I was born missing the largest bone you need to hear in my right ear so I've been half deaf my whole life

When I was 5 I was in a car accident and had to get staples in the back of my head with the scars still there

In the fourth grade, my best friend accidentally hit me in the mouth with a golf club and chipped my front tooth,
I'm still insecure about my smile today

In 9th grade I broke my foot, and my freshman year I separated my shoulder in my first college football game, so I can never quite shrug things off properly

Without my glasses I can hardly see,
I sometimes snort when things are too funny, and my social awkwardness at times has always been embedded into my personality

I have abandonment issues from growing up in an incomplete home where I felt like I always stuck out like a sore thumb no matter how much I hate attention

My first instinct has always been to laugh before I cry and sometimes I completely box everybody out and choose to internalize way more than anyone should

I've battled with depression, being overly self-conscious, and downplaying all my accomplishments while highlighting insecurities

I struggle with keeping relationships because I always think they'll up and leave so I second guess myself when opening up would really be best for me

So now that you know every insecurity I own,
hopefully you'll use it as a tool to understand why I am the way I am,
and not as a weapon against me.

Ready.

The truth is,
you'll never be completely ready.
When it's time to do something
in order to create change
it's usually never an ideal moment
that's placed in front of us
that encourages us to take that first step.
And those that learn
that we don't wait for opportunities
but instead create them,
those are the people
that find themselves
with constant opportunities
to elevate.
They're the ones that know
that in order to see the change,
they must first be the change.

ABOUT THE AUTHOR

Jarrin Wooten was born November 2nd, 1990 in Southern Pines, NC to DaShonda Wooten and Mario Lane. He is the oldest of 4 brothers and graduated from high school in 2009 and attended Winston-Salem State University, where he began to discover his love for writing and poetry. He graduated from WSSU in 2014 with a degree in elementary education, and currently resides in Charlotte, NC with his son Cameron where he has been a kindergarten teacher of 5 years. His long term aspirations are to eventually be able to travel and focus on creating more books for every age range. Jarrin is the author of the book **Skydive** and is set to release more books in the near future.

Made in the USA
Columbia, SC
08 July 2022